AF599131

COOL CARS

FERRARI ROMA

EPIC

BY KAITLYN DULING

BELLWETHER MEDIA ››› MINNEAPOLIS, MN

EPIC BOOKS are no ordinary books. They burst with intense action, high-speed heroics, and shadows of the unknown. Are you ready for an Epic adventure?

This edition first published in 2025 by Bellwether Media, Inc.

Library of Congress Cataloging-in-Publication Data

LC record for Ferrari Roma available at: https://lccn.loc.gov/2024002278

Editor: Rachael Barnes Designer: Jeffrey Kollock

Printed in the United States of America, North Mankato, MN.

TABLE OF CONTENTS

A GRAND TOUR

A Ferrari Roma rolls through Rome, Italy. It easily turns down narrow streets.

Then it heads for the highway. The Roma is a GT, or grand tourer. It is built for the open road!

WHEN IN ROMA

The Roma gets its name from Rome, Italy. The car is often called "the new sweet life" in Italian.

ALL ABOUT THE ROMA

ENZO FERRARI

Ferrari was formed by Enzo Ferrari. The company's first car came out in 1947.

Today, Ferrari makes race cars and GTs. The Portofino and 812 Superfast are famous GT **models**.

The Roma was announced in 2019. But it was first released as a 2021 model.

The Roma was built as a **supercar** for everyday drivers. It pairs simple, **retro** looks with modern power.

BLAST FROM THE PAST

The Roma's look took ideas from 1950s and 1960s cars. The 250 GT Berlinetta Lusso and the 250 GT 2+2 are two famous models from that time.

ROMA BASICS

YEAR FIRST MADE
2021
COST
starts around $243,000
HOW MANY MADE
currently being made
FEATURES
air intakes
grille
spoiler

PARTS OF THE ROMA

The Roma's long hood houses a **V8 engine**. The engine sends power to the rear wheels. **Air intakes** and a **grille** help keep the engine cool.

ENGINE SPECS

TWIN-TURBO V8 ENGINE

TOP SPEED	199 miles (320 kilometers) per hour
0-62 TIME	3.4 seconds
HORSEPOWER	612 hp

GRILLE
AIR INTAKE

The Roma's shape reduces **drag**. Its sharp nose cuts through the air. The smooth body helps air flow easily around the car.

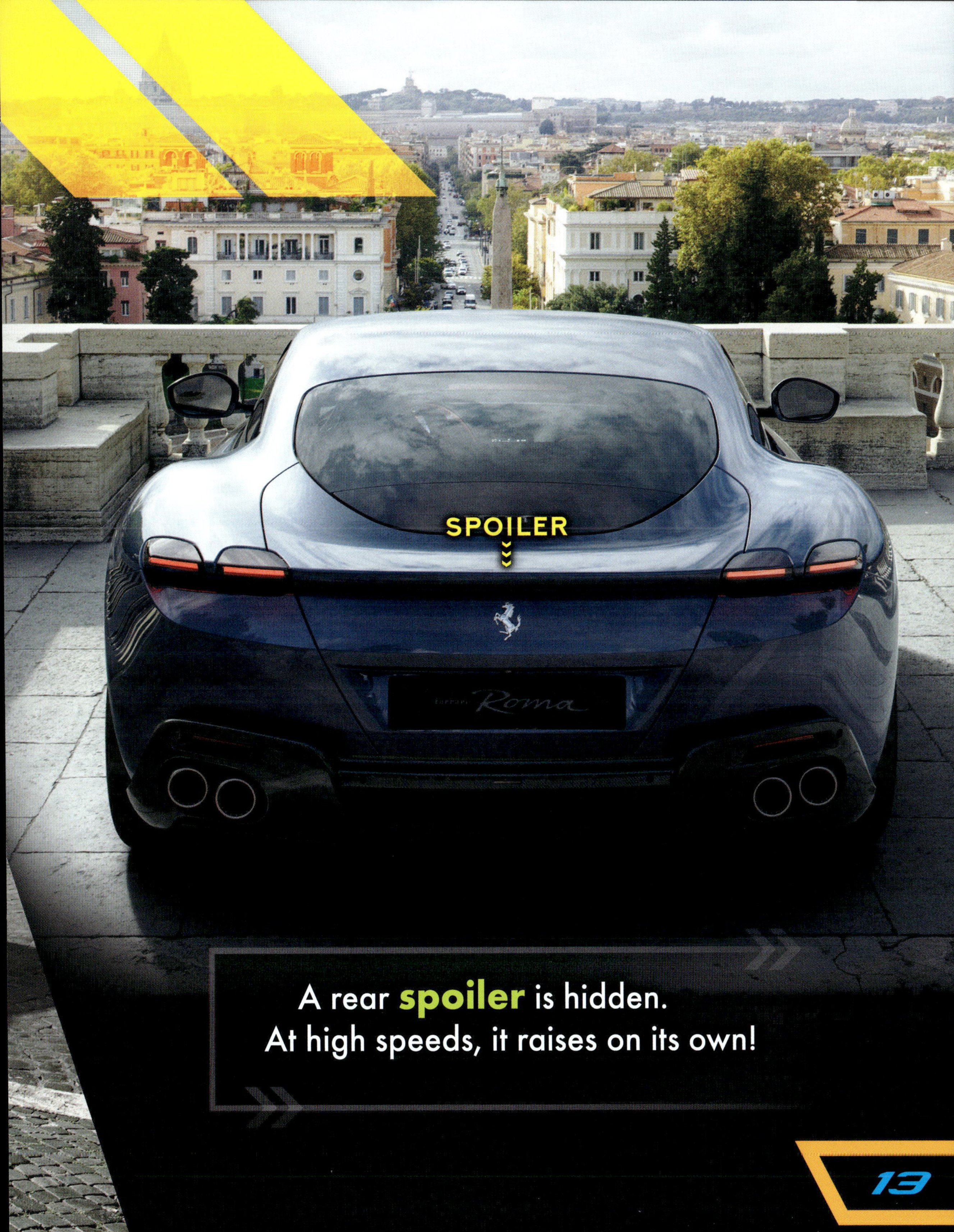

A rear **spoiler** is hidden.
At high speeds, it raises on its own!

Roma drivers can choose from five drive modes. The car starts in Sport mode. Wet mode is for rainy weather. Comfort mode offers the smoothest drive.

The Race and ESC-OFF modes are for expert drivers on the racetrack!

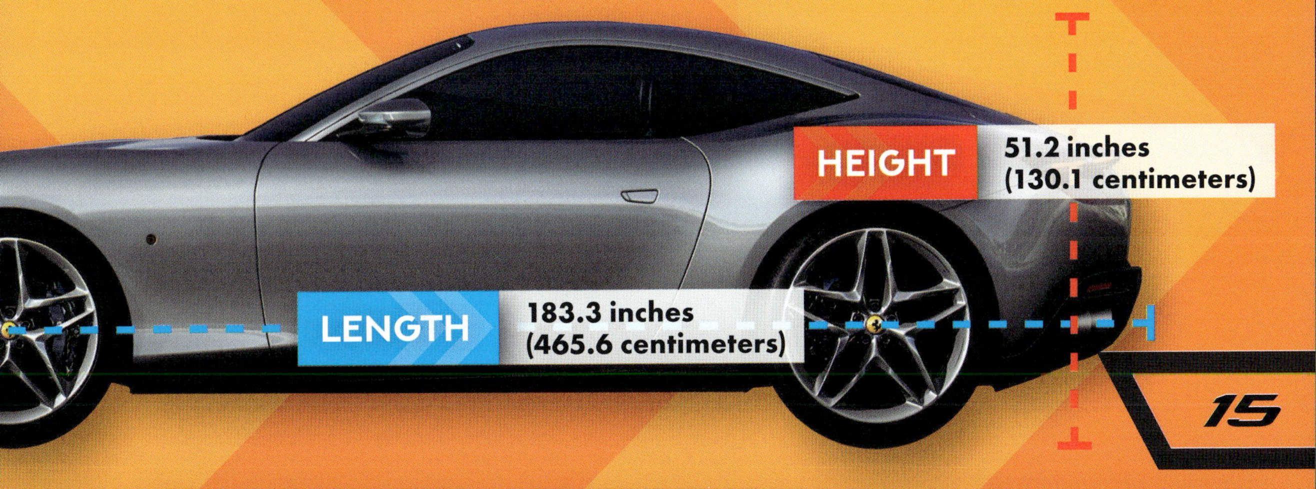

HEIGHT
51.2 inches
(130.1 centimeters)

LENGTH
183.3 inches
(465.6 centimeters)

The Roma is a two-door **coupe**. It has a very small backseat. Drivers start the engine with a button on the steering wheel.

The center **console** has three levers. Drivers use them to shift gears.

The Ferrari Roma Spider was introduced in 2023. It is a **convertible**.

The Spider's roof is made of fabric. It can move while the car is driving. It raises or lowers in just 13.5 seconds!

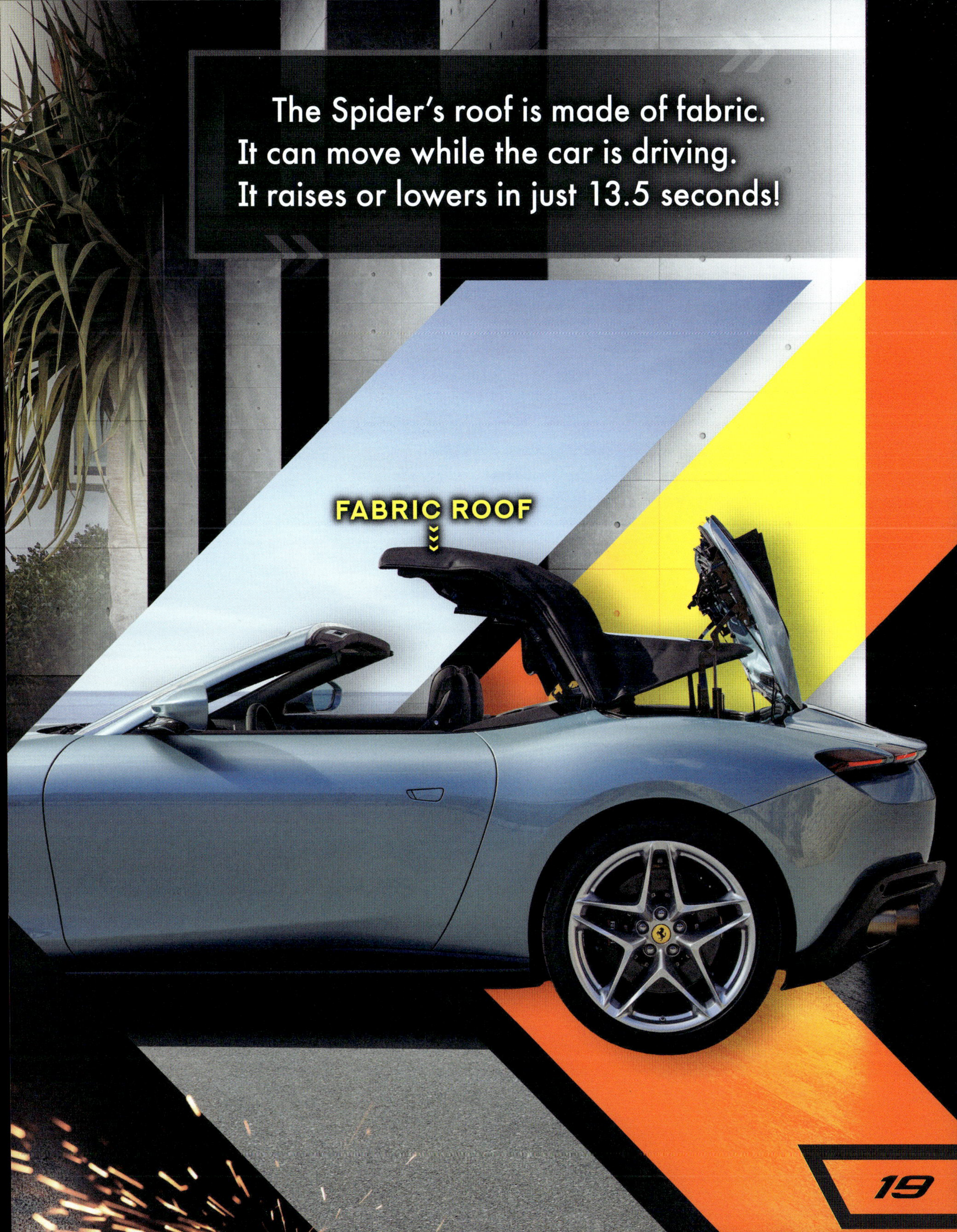

THE ROMA'S FUTURE

The Ferrari Roma is a standout model. In the future, the company plans to release many new cars. Some will be **hybrid** or **electric**.

Ferrari will keep building powerful cars. Fans will have many exciting options!

HYBRID RACE CAR

GLOSSARY

air intakes—openings on a car that allow air to reach its engine

console—the surface in a car that holds controls

convertible—a car with a folding or soft roof

coupe—a smaller car with a hard roof; coupes usually have two doors.

drag—a force that slows down an object; drag causes a car to go slower.

electric—able to run without gasoline

grille—a set of bars that cover an opening on the front of a car; the grille allows air to enter and exit.

hybrid—related to a car that uses both a gasoline engine and an electric motor for power

models—specific kinds of cars

retro—related to past styles or looks

spoiler—a part on the back of a car that helps a car grip the road

supercar—an expensive and high-performing sports car

V8 engine—an engine with 8 cylinders arranged in the shape of a "V"

TO LEARN MORE

AT THE LIBRARY

Duling, Kaitlyn. *Ferrari 296 GTB*. Minneapolis, Minn.: Bellwether Media, 2024.

Hamilton, S.L. *Ferrari*. Minneapolis, Minn.: Abdo Publishing, 2023.

Sommer, Nathan. *Ferrari 812 Superfast*. Minneapolis, Minn.: Bellwether Media, 2023.

ON THE WEB

FACTSURFER

Factsurfer.com gives you a safe, fun way to find more information.

1. Go to www.factsurfer.com.
2. Enter "Ferrari Roma" into the search box and click 🔍.
3. Select your book cover to see a list of related content.

INDEX

The images in this book are reproduced through the courtesy of: Ferrari, front cover, pp. 3, 4, 5, 6 (main), 8, 9 (isolated and spoiler), 10, 12, 13, 14 (main and width), 15 (length), 16, 17, 18, 19, 20, 21; Unknown/ Wikipedia, p. 6 (Enzo); Brandon Woyshnis, p. 7; Gabo_Arts, p. 9 (grille and air intakes); Jack Skeens, p. 11; Uwe Deffner/ Alamy, p. 15.